Retro Food Fiascos

A Collection of Curious Concoctions

Introduction &
Commentary
by Kathy Casey

PORTLAND, OREGON

Design: Wade Daughtry, Collectors Press, Inc.
Editors: Lisa Perry and Jennifer Weaver-Neist

Library of Congress Cataloging-in-Publication Data

Casey, Kathy.
  Retro food fiascos : a collection of curious concoctions /
Kathy Casey.-- 1st American ed.
     p. cm. -- (Retro series)
  ISBN 1-888054-88-3 (hardcover : alk. paper)
  1. Cookery, American. I. Title. II. Series.
TX715.C4253 2004
641.5973--dc22

                              2003023298

Printed in Singapore

9 8 7 6 5 4 3 2 1

Collectors Press books are available at special discounts for bulk
purchases, premiums, and promotions. Special editions, including
personalized inserts or covers, and corporate logos, can be printed in
quantity for special purposes. For further information contact:
Special Sales, Collectors Press, Inc., P.O. Box 230986, Portland, OR 97281.
Toll free: 1-800-423-1848.

For a free catalog write: Collectors Press, Inc., P.O. Box 230986,
Portland, OR 97281. Toll free: 1-800-423-1848 or visit our website at:
www.collectorspress.com.

Contents

introduction

Back in the "retro" days, when a woman's accomplishments were measured by the happiness of her family and being a good wife meant being a better cook, everything was molded, loafed, rolled, whipped, frosted, cut-out, skewered on a frill pick, and garnished with a bologna lily. Today's good cooks can be male or female and the measure of their success is based more upon good flavor than kooky, colorful, overly garnished concoctions. From multi-tiered gelatin molds to liver bonbons, we've come a long way, baby! (Thank goodness.)

While we laugh at, mock, and are sometimes disgusted by yesteryear's "modern" American recipes, the preparation of canned, sliced meats and wiener rolls was a serious business. It was no small feat to make sure your family meal included all seven food groups: (1) vegetables; (2) citrus fruits, tomatoes; (3) potatoes, other vegetables, fruits; (4) milk, cheese, ice cream; (5) meat, fish poultry, dried peas, beans, lentils; (6) bread, other flour products, cereals; (7) butter, margarine, fats, oils. I think the vegetable category mostly meant tomato soup, stuffed green olives, sauerkraut, and Veg-All (a can of mixed vegetables) in almost everything. So, when in doubt, they shoved all the groups into some flavored gelatin and molded it! (Hallelujah! The times, they are a-changin'!)

Today's cook has it easy, what with the detailed nutrition labels plastered on virtually every item and contemporary supermarkets providing endless aisles of groceries touting flavors, spices, and seasonings our grandmothers never dreamed of putting in their mouths. In the 1950s, going out to eat was a treat, Spam on a stick was the latest trend in culinary arts, and the big question in the kitchen was to mold or loaf. Today, eating out is a common part of everyday life, chefs will be damned if their meals don't include farmer's-market-fresh products, and the question of the day is organic or not organic.

So, why the continued fascination with meals that wiggle, meat and fruit loaves, not-so-sweet tomato soup cakes, and things in a can? Because, whether we hate it or love it, it is comfort food and a significant flavor memory. No matter where you are from within the United States, there is always going to be some dish that makes you squirm with distaste or squeal with delight. For me, the flavor memory that's most resonant on my tongue is...salmon loaf. Forget squirming, it makes me scream (and not in delight)! Made from salmon in a can – with the bones still in – and molded into a lovely loaf, I was told the bones were good for me and gave me extra calcium. Mmm, crunchy!

But I have good flavor memories too. I remember my mom's parties. She served the latest and greatest wacky appetizers, like smoked oysters and grapes skewered on a frilly pick. This was an age where people were experimenting with color and bringing some fun into their meals. Imagine eating the following ultra creative mold in a contemporary restaurant: lime Jell-O, sour cream, pineapple, walnuts, pimento-stuffed olives, and cottage cheese. Makes you wonder if this wasn't a time of heavy drinking in the kitchen.

Influenced by the 1960s era and colorful cookbooks with everything garnished like a fantasyland, I was a big experimenter in the kitchen. I used to make a pear bunny salad comprised of a bed of shredded lettuce for grass, almond ears, maraschino cherries for the nose, cherry stem tail, raisin eyes, and grated cheddar fur! I loved it – and it tasted yummy because it was cute and, of course, because I made it.

But the thing I liked to make most was really COLORFUL cookies. Frosted with fluorescent green and blue and lots of sparkles, these were the special cookies I set out for Santa. Sadly, I discovered that there was no physical Santa when I found my lovely, handmade cookie treasures back in the cookie tin the next day. (Mommy, reindeers really can fly, can't they?!?)

Retro Food Fiascos: A Collection of Curious Concoctions is a great tongue-in-cheek book poking friendly fun at America's past recipe creations, our grandmother's "secret" gelatin recipes, and the amazing combinations of things we used to put in our mouths. The evolution of kitchen culture is a fascinating, if not always tasty, culinary adventure. It's one that makes me grateful for balsamic roasted beets, arugula, readily available fresh herbs, and farmer's markets but thankful that I can still get a damn fine tube steak at the ball park or nibble a new and improved chipotle deviled egg with a dry martini at a cocktail party. (I'll take mine with gin and an olive, thank you.... Frill picks for this are approved!) Without the past we would not have such a delicious future, and I'd be willing to eat salmon loaf to that!

1

Appetizers, Teasers, Pupus, & Hors d'oeuvres

Deviled Delights

In the palm of your hand, pat out a little Deviled Ham; mold it around a stuffed olive, top with parsley sprigs, and spike with a toothpick. Delightful!

Ham it up!
Ham, Ma'am

11

Zesty Frankfurters

frankfurters
pickled onions
head of green cabbage
barbecue sauce
zippy cheese sauce (such as Cheez
   Whiz)

Cut frankfurters into 1-inch pieces.
Put each piece of frankfurter on a
pick; top with a pickled onion, kabob
style. Stick frankfurter picks into
the cabbage. Serve on tray with
bowls of barbecue and cheese
sauces.

Frankfurters, wieners, hotdogs,

a.k.a. tube steak – they're everywhere!

Does your man have a

wiener on his plate?

Bologna Lilies

Cut thin bologna slices into 2-inch circles. Fold each bologna circle, then insert a thin strip of pickle to represent the stamen of a lily. Fasten at the base with a pick. Refrigerate until served.

As if shaping bologna into a lily blossom would make it taste better. Your guests will squeal, "Ahhh, it's too pretty to eat!" No need for a centerpiece here!

My bologna used to have a first name...

Deviled Ham and Stuffed Olive Canapes

loaf of bread
1 small can deviled ham
1/4 cup nuts, chopped
2 tbsps butter, softened
slices of olives stuffed with pimientos

Cut bread in thin slices, remove crusts, and form
into shapes with a cutter. Mix ham, nuts, and butter
together and spread on bread. Arrange olive
slices on top.

Deviled road apples?

Liver-Sausage Pineapple

1 pound liver sausage
1 tbsp lemon juice
1 tsp Worcestershire sauce
1 1/4 cup mayonnaise, divided
2 tsps unflavored gelatin
2 tbsps cold water
stuffed olives, sliced

Mix together sausage, lemon juice,
Worcestershire sauce and 1/4 cup
mayonnaise. Shape around a jelly
glass. Soften gelatin in cold water
and dissolve over hot water. Add
in remaining 1 cup mayonnaise and
chill. Frost "pineapple," score;
stud with sliced, stuffed olives.
Top with real pineapple greens.

That's a pineapple that
would make Sponge Bob
Squarepants™ proud!
"Oh, he lives in a pineapple
under the sea..."

Stuff
-a-
Molé

Speedy Tuna Dunk

1/2 cup butter or margarine, softened
1/4 cup stuffed olives, chopped
1 can (1 cup) chunk-style tuna

Cream butter with olives and tuna until well
blended. Serve with dippers.

Mmm, mmm good...butter
and tuna fizz, creamy
smooth and oh-so-good
for you. Remember: butter
is one of the seven food
groups!

(Here kitty, kitty...)

Aspic Canapes

2 pkgs unflavored gelatin
2 cans (10 1/2 oz. each) condensed beef broth
1 cup Madeira wine
1/4 tsp Tabasco
24 hard-cooked egg slices
24 toasted bread rounds

Sprinkle gelatin on 1 cup of the beef broth to soften. Place over low heat and stir until the gelatin is dissolved. Remove from heat and stir in remaining broth, wine, and Tabasco. Pour half of the mixture into a 15 x 10 x 1-inch pan or 2 8-inch square pans. Chill mixture in refrigerator until almost firm. Arrange egg slices 1 inch apart in jelly. Spoon on remaining jelly, keeping egg slices in place and covered with aspic. Chill until firm. Cut into rounds, leaving an aspic edge on each slice. Place on toast rounds cut to same size and serve. Makes about 18.

Beef Jell-O...what more needs to be said?
If your husband doesn't come home on time,
I guess this is what you make for dinner.

Dried Beef Rolls

To a 3-oz. package of cream cheese, add one half of a finely chopped onion. Mix together thoroughly. Roll a strip of dried beef around a small amount of the cheese mixture. Fasten together with a wooden toothpick.

Sara, Tommy, Dad!
Hurry before someone
eats all the **beef rolls!**

Meat and Dill Slices

3 large dill pickles, 5 to 6 inches long
3/4 cup ground, cooked beef
1 hard-cooked egg, finely chopped
1 tbsp parsley, minced
1 tsp Worcestershire sauce
1/4 tsp monosodium glutamate
1/4 tsp salt
few grains Cayenne pepper
2 tbsps ketchup

Cut ends off pickles and cut crosswise into halves. Hollow out centers with apple corer and set pickles aside to drain thoroughly. Mix lightly with beef the egg, parsley, Worcestershire, monosodium glutamate, salt and Cayenne pepper. Moisten to a heavy paste with ketchup. Pack meat mixture into pickles and place in refrigerator to chill. Cut crosswise into 1/2-inch slices. Makes 30 to 36 slices.

Variation:
Instead of pickles, try 10 tiny, drained pickled beets. Add to meat mixture 1 teaspoon horseradish. Omit slicing.

How did Cher get in this book? Remember the pick and garnish-a-thon meals made by her character in the movie *Mermaids*? I guess it's true: if you pick it with a stick or stick it on a pick, it makes a mouth happy.

Making the wife's job easier:

canned and processed foods.

If you can open it, you can cook it.

Sausage-Filled Prunes

1 1/2 cups cooked prunes
1 pound bulk sausage
1/2 cup green sweet pepper, finely chopped
1/4 cup parsley, finely chopped
1 hard-cooked egg

Slit prunes on one side and remove pits. Fry sausage
and break into small pieces; drain off the fat. Mix
sausage with green pepper and parsley. Fill prunes with
the mixture and lay in a greased pan. Dot the top of
each with about 1/2 teaspoon of the sausage fat. Bake
10 minutes in a moderate oven (375 degrees). Press the
yolk and white of egg through a sieve separately and
garnish prunes after removing from oven. Serve hot.
Platter may be garnished with thin rings of pepper and
a prune placed in each. Allow 4 prunes to a serving.
Serves about 6.

Ahhh, Prunes are definitely the way to reLAX!
Prunes-Prunes,
the magical fruit: the more you eat, the more you toot!

Liver-Sausage BonBons

1 pound liver sausage
4 slices crumbled, crisp bacon
2 tbsps chopped chives or 1 tsp grated onion
1/3 cup chopped ripe or stuffed olives

Mash 1 pound liver sausage with a fork and add 4 slices crumbled crisp bacon, 2 tablespoons chopped chives, or 1 teaspoon grated onion; 1/3 cup chopped ripe or stuffed olives. Mix and shape into small balls. Dip into undiluted evaporated milk and then into cornflake crumbs. Fry in preheated shortening at 375 degrees about 2 minutes until brown. Drain on absorbent paper. Serve piping hot in little paper bonbon cases. Sprinkle with finely chopped parsley.

Oh Frank, you're such a hunk-o-burning grill man!

Soups & Salads

2

Eat Your Greens

&

Sip Your Soup

Yerba Buena Salad

1/2 cup pitted, ripe olives
1 tbsp green sweet pepper, chopped
1 tbsp green onion, chopped
1 cup cottage cheese, cream style
salt
4 medium-sized tomatoes

Cut olives into large pieces. Stir olives, pepper, and onion into cottage cheese. Salt to taste. Peel and core tomatoes; cut into halves crosswise. Put halves together with filling of cheese mixture. Serve on salad greens and top with parsley sprig. Serves 4.

The most green this salad has seen is the trio of olives, pepper, and green onion.
If it's garnished with parsley, it must be a salad!

Cucumber ice Salad

16 (1/4 pound) marshmallows, cut
1/3 cup lemon juice
2 medium-size cucumbers, grated (enough to yield
   2 cups pulp)
1 tsp onion, grated
1/2 tsp salt
3 drops green food coloring
few grains cayenne pepper
2 egg whites
1 tbsp sugar
8 medium-size tomatoes

Chill a bowl in refrigerator.

Heat together marshmallows and lemon juice in top of a double boiler, stirring occasionally until marshmallows are melted. Meanwhile, rinse, pare, and cut cucumbers into halves lengthwise and remove seeds. Mix grated cucumbers with onion, salt, food coloring, and cayenne pepper. Remove marshmallow mixture from simmering water; blend in cucumber mixture. Pour into a refrigerator tray. Place in freezing compartment of refrigerator and freeze until mixture is mush-like in consistency. Beat the egg whites until frothy. Add sugar and beat until rounded peaks are formed. Turn frozen mixture into the chilled bowl and beat with rotary beater. Spread egg whites over cucumber mixture and fold together. Immediately return mixture to refrigerator tray and freeze until firm, about 4 hours. Meanwhile, rinse and cut 1/2-inch slices from tops of tomatoes. Remove pulp with a spoon and invert the shells. Place in refrigerator to drain and chill while cucumber mixture is freezing. To serve, fill the tomato shells with Cucumber Ice and serve at once on chilled salad plates. Serves 8.

if it fits, stuff it, and if it isn't beaten, then it shouldn't be eaten.

Soup 'n' Salad

1 can (10 3/4 oz.) tomato soup
1/2 soup can (5 oz.) vegetable oil
1/2 soup can (5 oz.) vinegar
salt, pepper, and sugar to taste

In a quart jar, combine all ingredients.
Serve over any salad greens, fruit,
garden veggies! Season with cheese,
onion, chili powder, or other spices if
desired. Makes 2 1/2 cups.

Mackerel Soup

2 cups tomato juice
1 cube beef bouillon
1/2 medium cucumber, chopped
1 tbsps dry onion flakes
1/2 tsp basil leaves
8 oz. canned mackerel, drained

Combine all ingredients, except mackerel, in a saucepan. Cook over low heat, stirring frequently, 15 minutes or just until mixture comes to a boil. Add mackerel. Cook 4 minutes longer. Serves 2.

Holy SOUP – what a MACKEREL!

Whipped Peanut Butter Dressing

1/4 cup peanut butter
1 egg
1/2 tsp sugar
1 tsp salt
1/4 tsp pepper
2/3 cup peanut oil
1/4 cup lemon juice

Beat peanut butter, egg, sugar, salt, and pepper together with a rotary beater. Add peanut oil a little at a time, beating constantly until a thick mixture forms. When very thick, beat in lemon juice. Add any remaining oil, beating until well blended. Makes 1 1/3 cups.

Whip It, Whip It Good!

EASY-DO Variations

Celery Seed Dressing
To 1/2 cup of dressing, add 2 teaspoons sugar, 1/4 teaspoon celery seed, and 1 tablespoon catsup. Rub 4 butter-type crackers with garlic and crumble into dressing. (For fruit or green salads, too.)

Chili Dressing
To 1/2 cup of dressing, add 1/2 teaspoon sugar and 2 tablespoons chili sauce. (For greens, meat, or seafood salads.)

Man-Winner Tomato Salad With 1-Minute French Dressing

6 red-ripe tomatoes, cut into wedges or slices
1 onion, chopped
parsley to taste
2 tbsps capers (optional)

Top tomato wedges/slices with onion, parsley, and capers. Your dressing is 1-minute quick – and you can vary it so easily. So even this simple tomato salad has new surprise-flavor every day.

1-Minute French Dressing
1/2 tsp salt
1/4 tsp sugar
1/8 tsp pepper
1/8 tsp paprika
2 tbsps vinegar or lemon juice
1/3 cup oil

Shake all ingredients together in a covered jar. Shake before serving. Makes 1/2 cup.

Chicken Noodle Soup Salad

1 can chicken noodle soup
1 (3 oz.) pkg lemon Jell-O
3/4 cup boiling water
1 (6 1/2 oz.) can Hormel chicken
1/2 cup green onions, chopped fine
2 tbsps green pepper, chopped fine
1 cup chopped celery
1/2 cup mayonnaise
1/2 cup whipped cream, Cool Whip

Cut up noodles in soup. Dissolve Jell-O with water. Add remaining ingredients except mayonnaise and whip cream. When cool and set up a little, add mayonnaise and cream. For 8 x 8 pan, double for 9 x 13 pan.

Topping for 9 x 13 pan:
1 can tomato soup
1 pkg lemon Jell-O
1 cup boiling water

Combine ingredients, cool, and spread on top of salad.

Say, "Ahhh!"

This salad recipe was given to me in a regional, spiral-bound cookbook. I thought it would be the perfect addition for this book because it encompasses all the components to the perfect retro recipe fiasco: Jell-O, canned meat, mayonnaise, a fluffy sweet component, Jell-O "frosting," and, of course, garnishes galore. It was such a weird recipe we couldn't resist making it. And, yes, it tastes as weird as it sounds!

Pretzel Asparagus Salad

1 cup salad greens
6 canned or fresh asparagus stalks, cooked and chilled
1 hard-cooked egg
mayonnaise
1/2 to 3/4 pimiento, cut into strips
1/2 cup coarsely crushed pretzels

Arrange greens on individual plate. Top with asparagus. Place sliced, hard-cooked egg around asparagus; dot with mayonnaise. Decorate with the pimiento strips. Lastly, sprinkle pretzel crumbs over salad. Serve with French or any other salad dressing.
Serves 1

Famous Pennsylvania Pretzel Soup

A traditional recipe – delicious and quickly made.

2 (or more) pretzels
boiling water
1/2 tsp butter
1 cup hot milk
salt and pepper to taste

Break pretzels into a small, deep dish. Add boiling water to cover contents and steep, covered, for about a minute. Pour off water. Add butter and hot milk. Season and serve. Serves 1.

Ahhh...the essence of Coke

i don't know about you, but i prefer the un-cola!

French Onion Soup With Coke

1/4 cup butter or margarine
4 cups onions, thinly sliced
2 10 1/2 oz. cans beef broth or bouillon
3/4 cup Coca-Cola
1 tsp salt
1/2 tsp vinegar
1/8 tsp pepper
French bread, cut into thick slices
Parmesan cheese, grated

Melt the butter/margarine in a saucepan; add onions and cook until golden in color (do not brown). Add beef broth, 1 soup can of water, Coca-Cola, salt, vinegar, and pepper. Cover and let simmer for about 25 minutes. Toast one side of French bread slices under a hot broiler. Turn slices over, sprinkle Parmesan cheese on generously, and toast until browned. Ladle the soup into deep bowls and top with toast, cheese side up. Serves 4.

No, you may not pierce your tongue!

Nippy Cheese Freeze Salad

3 oz. natural cheese food (like Velveeta)
1/2 cup thick sour cream
8 to 10 stuffed olives, chopped
1 tsp lemon juice
1/4 tsp monosodium glutamate
3 drops Tabasco
salad greens
French dressing

Put cheese in a small bowl and mash with a fork. Add sour cream gradually, blending until mixture is smooth. Mix in the chopped olives, lemon juice, monosodium glutamate, and Tabasco. Turn mixture into refrigerator tray. Put into freezing compartment of refrigerator and freeze until mixture is firm. Cut the frozen cheese mixture into small cubes. Put chilled greens into a salad bowl and toss lightly with dressing. Add the cheese cubes and toss just enough to distribute the cubes evenly throughout the greens and serve immediately.
Serves 6 to 8.

Christmas Candle

1 slice of pineapple
1 banana
section of Brazil nut

Place the slice of pineapple on a salad plate. Cut off ends of banana so that the straight center section is approximately 4 inches long. Place this section upright in the ring of the pineapple. Cut a section of Brazil nut lengthwise and stick into top of banana for the wick of the candle. Garnish with crisp endive or lettuce. When ready to serve, light the Brazil nut. Dressing of your choice for this salad may be served separately. Serves 1.

Never knew you could light a Brazil nut. Twinkle, Twinkle little... Brazil nut?

Orange Jell-O With Pretzel Crust

2 1/2 cups pretzels (broken up)
3 tbsps sugar
3/4 cup melted margarine
6 oz. orange Jell-O
20 oz. crushed pineapple
8 oz. Cool Whip
8 oz. cream cheese
1 cup sugar

Toss first 3 ingredients together. Pour into oven-proof 13 X 9-inch baking dish and bake at 350 degrees for 10 minutes. Make Jell-O according to directions. Add drained pineapple. Mix cream cheese, 1 cup sugar, and Cool Whip together. Spread over pretzel crust. When partially set up, pour Jell-O over cool whip mixture. Place back in refrigerator to let Jell-O finish setting up.

a traditional Italian dish
goes *American*...

... and what happens is pure eating bliss! When it's as easy to fix as our "Yankee Doodle Pizza Pie," you'll shout "Bravo!" ... and your family will clamor for "Encores"! The savory filling is Ann Page Beans. Like all Ann Page Foods, they're made of choice ingredients in A&P's own Ann Page Kitchens ... sold only in A&P stores. This eliminates unnecessary in-between expenses and you share the saving. Adapted from Italy's regional cookery, this zesty dish is grand for parties ... and for downright All-American good eating *any* time!

PORK AND
BEANS
IN TOMATO SAUCE

MEATLESS
SPAGHETTI SAUCE

Yankee Doodle Pizza Pie

Pizza sauce
Blend together 1 (8 oz.) can ANN PAGE Spaghetti Sauce, 1 (7 oz.) can tomato paste, and ¼ teaspoon orégano.

Quick crust
Take one package refrigerator biscuits, separate them and press, pat and flatten to line one 12-inch pizza pan (round or square shallow baking pan may be used). Scallop the edge or make a rim.

To put together
Spread about 1½ cups sauce over crust, sprinkle on ½ cup grated Parmesan cheese. Add remaining sauce to one can (21 to 23 ozs.) of ANN PAGE BEANS (any style) pour over cheese layer. Decorate center with ¼ pound grated Mozarrella cheese and green pepper rings. Bake in hot oven (425°F.) 10 minutes; then at 325 degrees for 20-25 minutes more. Serve with Italian sausage, mushrooms, pimento, or anchovy.

Hawaiian Sandwich

How to create it thriftily: Make your salad from chicken or turkey leftovers – stretched, if need be, with a little boiled, diced veal. Serve the salad sandwich-style between sun-gold circles of luscious pineapple. Top them with a sliver of scarlet pimiento around crispy, toasted almonds. It's traditional party salad turned into a thriller!

This is definitely a dish worthy of the hostess with the mostess! The symbol for hospitality in colonial days, the pineapple represented the formidable rank, class, and resourcefulness of the hostess serving it. And after all, what says 'welcome' more than boiled, diced veal stuffed between two canned pineapple slices?

Things That Wiggle

Mustard Relish Molds

1 envelope unflavored gelatin
1 cup water
1/3 cup mayonnaise
1 cup mustard pickle relish
1/2 cup green pepper, finely diced
2 tbsps onion, finely chopped
1 cup celery, finely diced

Sprinkle gelatin on water to soften. Place over low heat and stir until gelatin is dissolved. Remove from heat and stir into mayonnaise. Chill to unbeaten egg white consistency. Fold in remaining ingredients. Turn into a 4-cup mold or individual molds and chill until firm. Unmold and garnish with watercress or serve individual molds on sliced tomato. Serves 6 to 8.

"There's always room for Jell-O!"

Red-Pine Salad

2 tbsps unflavored gelatin
1/2 cup water
1 20 1/2-oz. can crushed pineapple,
   drained, reserving juice
1 cup ketchup
1 tbsp vinegar
1 cup celery, chopped
chopped nuts, optional

Soften gelatin in the water. Add water to
reserved pineapple juice to make 2 cups;
heat. Dissolve gelatin in hot syrup; add
ketchup and vinegar. Chill. Fold in pineapple
and celery. Pour into 1-quart ring mold; chill.
Unmold; top with chopped nuts. Serves 8.

Ring-Around-the-Tuna

1 pkg (3 oz.) Jello-O lime or lemon gelatin
1/4 tsp salt
1 cup boiling water
3/4 cup cold water
2 tbsps vinegar
2 tsps grated onion
1/2 cup diced cucumber
1/2 cup diced celery
2 tbsps chopped pimiento
2 tbsps stuffed olives, sliced
1 can (7 oz.) tuna, drained and flaked

Dissolve Jell-O gelatin and salt in boiling water. Add cold water, vinegar, and onion. Chill until very thick. Stir in remaining ingredients and pour into individual ring molds or a 1-quart ring mold. Chill until firm. Unmold onto crisp salad greens. If desired, serve with additional tuna and top salads with mayonnaise. Serves 4.

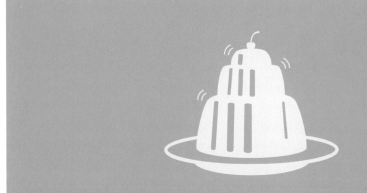

45

The chef's of the 1950s and 1960s were gelatin experts! Observe how even and perfectly suspended their pimento stuffed olives were! These cooks obviously knew that achieving maximum suspension required chilling the Jell-O to the consistency of cold egg whites before mixing in their meats, fruits, and vegetables.

Perfection Salad

2 envelopes (2 tbsps) unflavored gelatin
1/2 cup sugar
1 tsp salt
1 1/2 cups boiling water
1 1/2 cups cold water
1/2 cup vinegar
2 tbsps lemon juice
2 cups finely-shredded cabbage
1 cup chopped celery
1/2 cup chopped green pepper
1/4 cup chopped pimiento

Mix gelatin, sugar, and salt. Add boiling water and stir until gelatin dissolves. Add cold water, vinegar, and lemon juice; chill until partially set. Add vegetables; pour into 6 1/2-cup ring mold. Chill until firm. Unmold on greens, if desired, and fill ring with tiny, whole-cooked or canned carrots that have been marinated in French or Italian dressing overnight.

Olive trim:
Chill gelatin until partially set; pour 1/2 cup of gelatin into mold. Arrange trios of stuffed green olive slices in mold and chill until firm. Add vegetables to remaining gelatin and pour over. Chill until set. Serves 6 to 8.

Red Hot Salad

2 pkgs (3 oz. each) cherry gelatin
4 oz. Red Hots candy
3 cups boiling water
20 oz. crushed pineapple, undrained
2 cups applesauce

Dissolve gelatin and Red Hots (also known as Cinnamon Imperials) in boiling water. When cooled to room temperature, add pineapple and applesauce. Pour into oiled 8-cup mold. Chill before serving. Serves 6.

Ohh baby! it's spicy, hot, puffy, and jiggly with pink passion.

Lime and Cottage Cheese Loaf

1 pkg (3 oz.) lime gelatin
1 cup hot water
1 medium-size cucumber
1 cup cream-style cottage cheese
1/2 cup mayonnaise
1/3 cup ripe olives, sliced
2 tsp onion, grated
1/2 tsp salt
1/8 tsp white pepper
3 oz. cream cheese, softened
1 tbsp salad dressing
3/4 tsp grated onion
1/8 tsp salt

Set out a 9 1/2 x 5 1/4 x 2 3/4-inch loaf pan. In a bowl, mix the gelatin with hot water until gelatin is completely dissolved. Cool. Chill until mixture is slightly thicker than consistency of thick, unbeaten egg white. Lightly oil the pan with salad or cooking oil (not olive oil); set aside to drain. Rinse and pare the cucumber. Cut into halves lengthwise; remove and discard seeds. Dice the cucumber (enough to yield 1 cup, diced). Mix with cottage cheese, mayonnaise, olives, onion, salt, and pepper. When gelatin mixture is of desired consistency, blend in the cottage cheese mixture. Turn into the prepared pan and chill in refrigerator until firm. Meanwhile, mix together cream cheese, dressing, onion, and salt. Set in refrigerator to chill and to allow flavors to blend. To serve, unmold loaf onto a chilled serving plate and spread the cream cheese mixture over top of loaf. Serves 8.

Grapefruit-Lime Salad With Mixed Vegetables

1 pkg lime gelatin
1 pkg lemon gelatin
hot water
1 can mixed vegetables, drained
2 cups drained grapefruit segments

Mix gelatin with hot water according to package directions. Cool. Add grapefruit and 1 cup mixed vegetables. Chill in ring mold until firm. Serve on head lettuce. Fill center of ring with remaining mixed vegetables.

Sauerkraut Jell-O

1 packet of Jell-O (any flavor)
1 1/2 cups sauerkraut
1 cup cooked carrots
1 tsp water

Make Jell-O according to package.
Before Jell-O firms, add sauerkraut,
carrots, and water. Let it firm and
enjoy! It's lovely! Serves 3.

It would appear that American chefs took the 19th century Victorian tradition of food molds to a whole new level! Back then, pudding, ice cream, and jelly molds were indicative of class and sophistication. This recipe for molded entrée salad is the perfect excuse to get rid of last night's leftovers. But hey, if the mold fits...

Tomato Aspic Ring

2 envelopes unflavored gelatin
1/3 cup cold water
3 cups tomato juice
3 tbsps vinegar
1 small onion, sliced
1 rib celery with leaves, cut up
2 bay leaves
3 whole cloves
6 black peppercorns
1 tsp salt
1 tsp Worcestershire sauce
cayenne pepper
1 head iceberg lettuce, shredded

In a large bowl, sprinkle gelatin over cold water to soften. Combine tomato juice, vinegar, onion, celery, bay leaves, cloves, and peppercorns. Bring to a boil then simmer 5 minutes. Strain and add to gelatin. Stir in salt, Worcestershire, and a dash of cayenne. Pour into an oiled 1-quart ring mold. Refrigerate until aspic is firm, then unmold onto lettuce to serve. Serves 6 to 8.

Who's that salad for, lady?

Lemon-Olive Mold

1 pkg (3 oz.) lemon gelatin
1 cup hot water
1/4 cup mayonnaise
2 tbsps prepared mustard
1/2 cup ripe olives, chopped
3/4 cup celery, chopped
2 tbsps pimiento, chopped
2/3 cup (small can) undiluted evaporated milk
1 tbsp lemon juice

Dissolve gelatin in hot water. Chill to consistency of unbeaten egg white. Add mayonnaise, mustard, olives, celery, and pimiento. Freeze evaporated milk in refrigerator or freezer tray until soft ice crystals form around edges of tray (10-15 minutes). Whip until stiff, about 1 minute. Add lemon juice and whip very stiff, about 1 minute longer. Fold into gelatin mixture. Spoon into individual molds. Chill until set, about 2 hours. Unmold on salad greens. Great for a luncheon! Serve this with cold, sliced meats, hot rolls, and tall, frosty glasses of iced tea on warm days. Serves 8 to 10.

Vegetable Salad Loaf

2 pkgs (3 oz. each) lemon gelatin
3 1/2 cups hot water
1/2 tsp salt
2 tbsps vinegar
9 to 12 long green beans, cooked
3 to 4 long strips pimiento
1 small head cauliflower broken into small florets,
   cooked
1/2 cup carrots, sliced and cooked
1/4 cup diced celery
3 sliced radishes

Dissolve gelatin in hot water; add salt and
vinegar. Pour about 1/2 inch of gelatin mixture
into 8 1/2 x 4 1/2 x 2 1/2-inch loaf pan. Chill until
set. Arrange 3 to 4 bundles of 3 to 4 green
beans tied with pimiento strips on gelatin. Pour
more of gelatin cooled to room temperature in
pan until beans are covered. Chill until firm. Chill
remaining gelatin until slightly thickened; combine
with cauliflower, carrots, celery, and radishes.
Pour over first two layers. Chill. Serves 8.

Okay kids, eat your **veggies!**

Mom will disguise them in a lovely,

Jell-O mold. You won't even know that

what you are eating is good for you.

Garden Patch Salad

1 envelope unflavored gelatin
1/4 cup sugar
1/2 tsp salt
1 1/2 cups water, divided
1/4 cup lemon juice
2 cups mixed vegetables, cooked

Mix gelatin, sugar, and salt thoroughly in a small saucepan. Add 1/2 cup of the water. Place over low heat, stirring constantly until gelatin is dissolved. Remove from heat and stir in remaining 1 cup water and lemon juice. Chill mixture to unbeaten egg white consistency. Fold in mixed vegetables. Turn into a 3-cup mold or individual molds and chill until firm. Unmold on serving platter and garnish with salad greens, scallions, and radishes. Serves 6.

Spinach Mold

1 peck spinach, cooked tender and put
   through grinder
3 eggs
1/4 cup canned milk, undiluted
1/4 cup butter
1 1/2 cups bread crumbs
1/4 tsp pepper
1 tsp salt

Combine all ingredients, turn into a buttered
ring mold, and steam for 2 hours. Unmold and
garnish with hard-cooked eggs and carrots.
Fill the inside of the mold with mashed potatoes
or creamed mushrooms. Serves 6 to 8.

Spinach Mold...
i don't know.
it sure looks
like molded
mold to me.

Cottage Cheese and Kidney Bean Salad

1 1/2 cups cottage cheese
1 envelope unflavored gelatin
1 cup milk, divided
2/3 cup French dressing
1 tbsp minced onion
dash pepper
1 cup cooked or canned kidney beans, drained
1 cup cabbage, shredded

Sieve cheese or beat on high speed of electric mixer
for 3 minutes. Stir gelatin into 1/2 cup of the milk to
soften. Place over low heat, stirring constantly until
gelatin is dissolved. Remove from heat and stir in
remaining 1/2 cup milk, French dressing, onion, pepper,
and cottage cheese. Place pan in bowl of ice and water
or chill in refrigerator to unbeaten egg white
consistency. Fold in drained kidney beans and
shredded cabbage. Turn into a 4-cup mold and chill
until firm. Unmold by dipping mold in warm water to the
depth of the gelatin. Loosen around edge with tip of
paring knife. Place serving dish on mold; turn upside-
down. Shake, holding dish tightly to mold. Garnish with
greens and cucumbers. Serves 6 to 8.

Vegetable Salad

1 pkg (3 oz.) lemon, lime, orange, or orange-pineapple gelatin
3/4 tsp salt
1 cup boiling water
3/4 cup cold water
2 tbsps vinegar
2 tsps grated onion
dash of pepper
3/4 cup cabbage, finely chopped *
3/4 cup celery, finely chopped *
1/4 cup green pepper, finely chopped *
2 tbsps pimiento, diced *

*Or use any vegetable combination listed below

Dissolve gelatin and salt in boiling water. Add cold water, vinegar, onion, and pepper. Chill until very thick, then fold in vegetables. Pour into a 1-quart mold or individual molds. Chill until firm. Unmold and serve. Makes about 3 cups, 6 side salads, or 8 to 10 relish servings.

Other vegetable combinations:
Use 1 1/4 cups cauliflower florets and 1/4 cup diced pimiento.
Use 3/4 cup diced tomato and 1/2 cup each diced cucumber and celery.
Use 3/4 cup grated carrots and 1/4 cup finely chopped green pepper.
Use 1 1/2 cups finely chopped cabbage, 1/2 cup sliced stuffed olives, and 2 tbsps chopped parsley.
Use 1/2 cup each thinly sliced radishes and chopped celery and 1/4 cup thin onion rings.
Use 1 to 2 cups of your favorites.

This is one Jell-O chapeau that Audrey Hepburn would have loved to wear. The Coneheads would have enjoyed them, too!

56

Tomato-Relish Ring

You really won't know how good this salad can taste unless you try it with Miracle Whip Salad Dressing. For Miracle Whip has a lively "different" flavor no other kind can give you. Made by a secret recipe and mixed in a patented beater, it's a unique type of salad dressing, combining the qualities of zesty boiled dressing and fine mayonnaise. Watch your family go for the one and only Miracle Whip!

1 1/2 tbsps gelatin
2 1/4 cups tomato juice
1/2 tsp salt
Miracle Whip
3/4 cup India relish or chopped sweet pickle
lettuce
deviled eggs

Soften gelatin in 1/4 cup cold tomato juice. Dissolve in 2 cups heated tomato juice. Add salt. Chill. When semi-firm, fold in India relish or chopped sweet pickle. Pour into a 6 1/2-inch ring mold; chill until firm. Serve on lettuce, with deviled eggs. Fill center with lettuce and Miracle Whip Salad Dressing.

Sugarless Gazpacho Salad

2 tbsps unflavored gelatin
1/2 cup cold Diet Dr Pepper
1 1/2 cups (12-oz. can) hot tomato juice
1 1/2 tsps wine vinegar
1/8 tsp hot pepper sauce
6 large tomatoes, peeled, seeded, and finely
    chopped
1/3 cup green pepper, finely chopped
1 tsp salt
1/4 tsp pepper

Dissolve gelatin in the cold Diet Dr Pepper. Combine the gelatin with the tomato juice until partially congealed; add chopped vegetables and seasonings. Pour in seasoned gelatin mold. Chill until completely congealed; remove and garnish with your favorite salad dressing. Serve slices of salad on lettuce leaves. Serves 10.

Concocted in Waco, Texas, **Dr Pepper,** "the friendly Pepper-Upper" is the oldest of American soft drinks. Like its flavor, this recipe is out of the ordinary. But go ahead, cook it up, and "Be You, **Be a Pepper!**"

Sea Dream?

More like shrimp-infested

kryptonite.

Sea Dream Salad

1 pkg (3 oz.) Jell-O lime gelatin
1 1/4 cups boiling water
1 cup grated cucumber
1 tbsp vinegar
3/4 tsp grated onion
1/2 tsp salt
dash of cayenne
1 pound shrimp, cooked and cleaned

Dissolve Jell-O gelatin in boiling water. Add remaining ingredients, except shrimp; force through sieve. Pour into individual ring molds or a 3-cup or 1-quart ring mold. Chill until firm. Unmold on salad greens and fill rings with shrimp. Serves 4.

Vegetable Trio

2 pkgs (3 oz. each) or 1 pkg (6 oz.) lemon gelatin
1 tbsp salt
2 cups boiling water
2 cups cold water
2 tbsps vinegar
1 1/2 cups carrots, finely shredded
1 3/4 cups cabbage, finely shredded
1 tsp chives, minced
1 1/2 cups spinach, finely chopped

Dissolve gelatin and salt in boiling water. Add cold water and vinegar. Chill until slightly thickened. Divide into three portions. Fold carrots into one portion; pour into a 9 x 5 x 3-inch loaf pan. Chill until set but not firm. Fold cabbage into second portion. Pour into pan; chill until set but not firm. Fold chives and spinach into remaining gelatin. Pour into pan. Chill until firm. Unmold. Slice and garnish with crisp greens. Makes about 6 cups or 12 side salads.

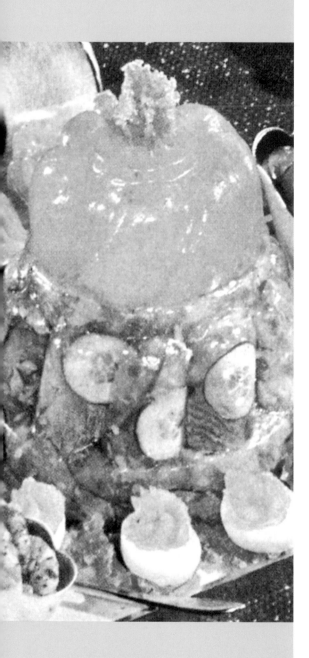

Lemony Salmon Tower

Tart, shimmery, lemon gelatin accents rich salmon flavor in this luscious molded salad. Cucumber, celery, and green pepper add crunch. Relishes are anchovies, herring in sour cream, marinated shrimp, sardines, pickled beets, and pickles.

Lemon layer:
1 envelope (1 tbsp) unflavored gelatin
1/4 cup cold water
1 cup boiling water
1 tbsp sugar
1/2 tsp salt
3 tbsps lemon juice
few drops yellow food coloring

Soften gelatin in cold water. Dissolve in boiling water.
Add sugar, salt, lemon juice, and add food coloring.
Pour into 2 1/2-quart mold. Chill until set.

Salmon-salad layer:
3 envelopes unflavored gelatin
3/4 cup cold water
3 1/4 cups boiling water
1/4 cup vinegar
1/4 cup lemon juice
1 1/2 tsps salt
2 1-pound cans (4 cups) red salmon, drained and broken in pieces
2 cups drained, canned, or cooked peas
1 1/2 cups celery, diced
1/2 cup green pepper strips
1/2 cup unpared cucumber, thinly sliced

Soften gelatin in cold water. Dissolve in boiling water. Add vinegar, lemon juice, and salt. Chill until partially set. Add salmon and vegetables; mix carefully. Pour over lemon layer. Chill until firm. Serves 12.

Jellied Grape Salad

2 pkgs (3 oz.) raspberry gelatin
dash salt
2 cups hot water
1 3/4 cups cold Dr Pepper
2 tbsps lemon juice
1 1/2 cups canned green grapes, drained
1 1/2 cups fruit cocktail, drained
1/3 cup fresh coconut, grated (optional)

Dissolve gelatin and salt in hot water. Cool and chill slightly. Stir in cold Dr Pepper and lemon juice. Chill until slightly thickened. Fold in fruits and coconut. Pour into 2-quart mold or individual molds that have been lightly greased. Chill until set. Frost with Cream Cheese Dressing (see below). Makes 1 (2-quart) mold or 12 to 16 individual salads.

Cream Cheese Dressing

Beat 6 ounces cream cheese until smooth. Gradually add Dr Pepper (1/4 cup) to make consistency for easy spreading.

Main Course 4

Dixie Bake

12-oz. can Spam
12 whole cloves
2 cups Bisquick
2/3 cup milk
1/2 cup apricot jam
1/2 tsp dry mustard
1 tbsp water

Preheat oven to 425 degrees. Slice Spam into 12 squares almost through to bottom. Stud with whole cloves. Place in 8-inch, square baking dish. Add milk all at once to Bisquick. Stir with fork. Beat 15 strokes. Roll dough around on cloth-covered board lightly dusted with Bisquick. Knead gently 10 times. Roll 1/2-inch thick. Makes about 12 2-inch biscuits. Surround meat with biscuits. Spread meat and biscuits with mixture of jam, mustard, and water. Bake 20 minutes until biscuits are golden.

Succulent Spam...
Made to look like a ham.
Poked with cloves,
They will feed in droves.
If you're feeling dazed,
Just top it with glaze
And you'll please your man
With some hearty canned Spam!

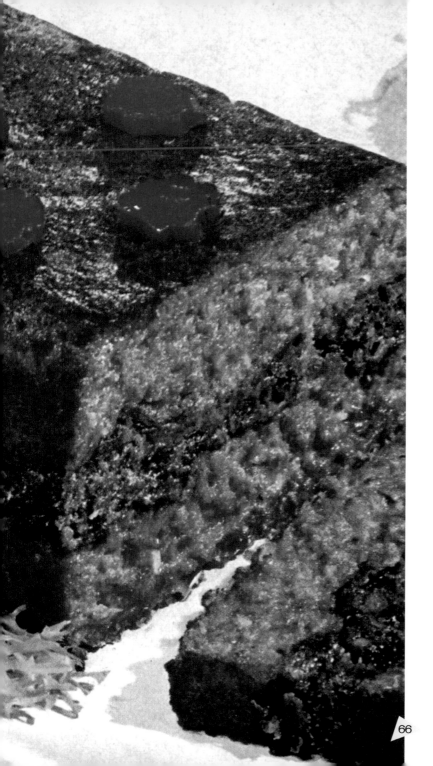

Heavenly Ham Loaf With Pickle Stuffing

Meat layer:
2 12-oz. cans luncheon meat
1/2 cups fine, dry bread crumbs
1/4 tsp pepper
1/4 tsp thyme
1/2 cup onion, finely chopped
2 eggs
2 cups evaporated milk

Pickle stuffing:
2 tsps prepared mustard
1/2 cup evaporated milk
1 cup fine, dry bread crumbs
1 1/4 cups sweet pickle relish

In mixing bowl, shred luncheon meat into bits by running tines of fork over meat. (Or put through food chopper using medium blade.) Add the 1/2 cup crumbs, seasonings, and onion. Mix thoroughly. Beat eggs slightly with a fork and add 2 cups evaporated milk. Add egg-milk mixture to meat mixture. Mix thoroughly. Pack half the meat mixture into well-greased loaf pan. For the pickle layer, stir mustard into 1/2 cup evaporated milk. Add 1 cup crumbs and pickle relish and blend. Spread pickle stuffing evenly and firmly on meat layer. Pack remaining half of meat mixture over pickle layer. Bake at 375 degrees for 1 hour and 15 minutes. Serves 10 to 12.

Jellied Moose Nose

1 upper jawbone of a moose
1 onion, sliced
1 garlic clove
1 tbsp pickling spice
1 tsp salt
1/2 tsp pepper
1/4 cup vinegar

Cut the upper jawbone of the moose just below the eyes. Place in a large kettle of scalding water and boil for 45 minutes. Remove and chill in cold water. Pull out all the hairs – these will have been loosened by the boiling and should come out easily like plucking a duck. Wash thoroughly until no hairs remain. Place the nose in a kettle and cover with fresh water. Add onion, garlic, spices, and vinegar. Bring to a boil, then reduce heat and simmer until the meat is tender. Let cool overnight in the liquid. When cool, take the meat out of the broth and remove and discard the bones and the cartilage. You will have two kinds of meat: white meat from the bulb of the nose and thin strips of dark meat from along the bones and jowls. Slice the meat thinly and alternate layers of white and dark meat in a loaf pan. Reheat the broth to boiling, then pour the broth over the meat in the loaf pan. Let cool until jelly has set. Slice and serve cold.

Summer Salad Pie

1 pkg (3 oz.) lemon-flavored gelatin
1 1/4 cups boiling water
1 can (8 oz.) tomato sauce
1 tbsp vinegar
1/2 tsp salt
few drops each of Worcestershire sauce and
    Tabasco
dash of pepper
1/2 cup each celery and pimiento-stuffed olives,
    chopped
1/4 cup onion, chopped
Cheese Pie Shell (see recipe)
Tuna Salad (see recipe)

Dissolve gelatin in boiling water. Stir in tomato sauce,
vinegar, and seasonings. Chill until slightly thickened.
Fold in celery, olives, and onion. Pour into cooled
Cheese Pie Shell. Chill thoroughly. Spoon Tuna Salad
on top of pie. Serves 6.

Cheese Pie Shell

1 cup flour
1/2 tsp salt
1/3 cup plus 1 tbsp shortening or 1/3 cup lard
1/2 cup sharp cheddar cheese, shredded
2 tbsps water

Preheat oven to 475 degrees. Mix flour and salt. Cut
in shortening thoroughly. Stir in cheese. Sprinkle
water gradually over mixture, 1 tablespoon at a time,
tossing lightly with a fork after each addition. (If
dough appears dry, a few drops of water may be
added.) Gather dough into a ball. On a lightly floured,
cloth-covered board, roll out 1 inch larger than
inverted 9-inch pie pan. Ease into pan; flute and
prick pastry. Bake 8 to 10 minutes; cool.

Tuna Salad

1 can (6 1/2 oz.) tuna, drained
1 tsp lemon juice
1 tsp onion, minced
1 cup celery, diced
salt
paprika
mayonnaise or salad dressing

Lightly mix tuna, lemon juice, onion, and celery.
Season with salt and paprika to taste. Chill. Just
before serving, drain and mix in just enough
mayonnaise to moisten.

Sweet Peas in Salmon Loaf Ring

1 can sweet peas
2 tbsps butter
1/2 tsp salt
1/3 cup liquid from peas
2 tbsps flour
2/3 cup milk
speck of pepper
salmon loaf

Bake your favorite salmon loaf in a ring mold pan. Melt butter in saucepan; add flour, pepper, and salt. Stir until blended. Add milk mixed with pea liquid gradually while stirring. Cook until smooth and thickened, stirring constantly. Turn salmon loaf onto a platter and fill center with hot, buttered peas. Serve sauce separately.

...from the mountains,
to the prairies,
to the ring molds filled with
peas, peas, peas...

Lemonade Fried Chicken

6 oz. frozen lemonade concentrate
1 cup water
2 1/2 pound fryer, cut up
1/4 cup flour, unbleached
1 tsp salt
1/4 tsp pepper
1 cup vegetable oil
2 tbsps butter, melted

Preheat oven to 350 degrees. Mix lemonade concentrate and water in a small bowl. Pour over chicken in larger bowl. Refrigerate 2 hours or longer. Drain chicken and reserve liquid. Mix together the flour, salt, and pepper in a small paper bag. Add well-drained chicken, one piece at a time, and shake to coat evenly. Heat oil in large skillet over moderate heat. Add floured chicken; cook until evenly browned, turning pieces over carefully. Remove chicken and arrange in a single layer in a shallow baking pan. Brush chicken with melted butter; add reserved lemonade. Bake uncovered about 1 hour, basting chicken with lemonade from pan every 15 minutes. About 15 minutes before chicken is done, drain off excess juice from pan. Serve hot. Serves 4.

Veal-Oyster Loaf

1/2 pint oysters, drained, bits of shell
   removed, finely chopped
1 pound ground veal
1 1/4 cups crushed corn flakes
1/2 cup (about 1 medium-size) onion, minced
3/4 cup evaporated milk, undiluted
1 egg, beaten
mixture of:
   3/4 tsp salt
   1/2 tsp monosodium glutamate
   1/4 tsp paprika
   1/4 tsp marjoram
   1/8 tsp thyme

Lightly mix together oysters, veal, corn flakes, onion, milk, eggs, and seasonings. Pack lightly into a greased 9 1/2 x 5 1/4 x 2 3/4-inch loaf pan. Bake at 350 degrees for about 1 1/2 hours. Unmold the loaf and serve with Swiss cheese slices. Garnish with parsley sprigs. Serves 6 to 8.

It's New! It's Easy!
TUNA PIZZA

Tuna Pizza

Heat oven to 450 degrees. Mix 1/2 cup PET Evaporated milk, 3/4 cup grated Parmesan cheese, and 1/2 teaspoon onion salt. Let stand to thicken. Arrange 1 can oven-ready biscuits close together on ungreased baking sheet. With fingers, press biscuits together to close spaces, making one big, thin biscuit-crust (about 12 inches across). Bake 5 minutes. Remove from oven and loosen crust with spatula. Leave on baking sheet. Spread cheese mixture almost to crust edge; cover with 1/2 cup tomato sauce or ketchup. Drain 1 can (7 oz.) tuna, break into large chunks, and arrange over top. Sprinkle with 1/2 teaspoon oregano. Return to oven for 7 minutes or until crust is brown. Serve hot. For variety: in place of tuna, try canned shrimp, sardines, anchovies, or mushrooms...or cooked sausage or hamburger...or strips of salami, thuringer, pepperoni, or bologna.

Oven Ready **Biscuits**

Bologna Biscuit Bake

1/4 cup sliced onion
2 tbsps shortening
2 tbsps flour
1/2 tsp salt
1/8 tsp pepper
1 can (2 cups) tomatoes
1/2 pound bologna, cubed (2 cups)
3/4 cup diced carrots, cooked and drained
3/4 cup cut green beans, cooked and drained
Bologna Biscuits (below)

Heat oven to 425 degrees. Cook and stir onion in hot shortening until tender. Remove from heat. Blend in flour, salt, and pepper. Cook over low heat, stirring until mixture is bubbly. Remove from heat. Stir in tomatoes. Heat to boiling, stirring constantly. Boil 1 minute. Add bologna, carrots, and beans; return to boiling. Pour into 8 x 8 x 2-inch square pan. Place in oven to keep hot while making Bologna Biscuits. Drop 8 or 9 tablespoonfuls of biscuit dough on hot mixture. Bake 25 to 30 minutes or until biscuits are lightly browned. Serves 5.

Bologna Biscuits
1 cup flour
1 1/2 tsps baking powder
1/2 tsp salt
2 tbsps shortening
1/4 pound bologna, cut into 1/4-inch cubes (1 cup)
1/2 cup milk

Mix flour, baking powder, and salt in bowl; cut in shortening with pastry blender until moisture looks like meal. Stir in bologna cubes then milk.

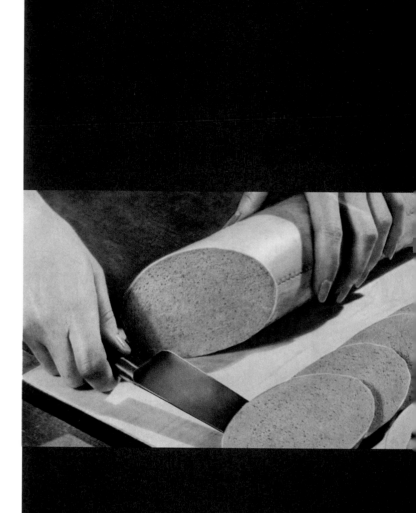

Bologna Biscuit Bake:
the perfect Sunday dish.
Slice it thin and pile it high,
then sit back and watch it fly.

Yum-m-m-m!

Turkey in a Stuffing Crust

6 cups stuffing mix
1 1/2 to 2 cups water
1/2 cup onion, chopped
1/2 cup celery, chopped
3 tbsps butter
1/4 cup flour
2 1/2 cups evaporated milk, undiluted
1/2 cup stuffed green olives, sliced
3 cups cooked turkey, cubed
1/4 tsp pepper
1/4 tsp thyme
1/8 tsp poultry seasoning

Combine stuffing mix with water, using only
enough liquid to moisten and mix well. Press
into buttered 12 x 7 1/2 x 2-inch baking dish.
Bake at 400 degrees for 10 minutes. Saute
onion and celery in butter; add flour. Blend
well then gradually stir in milk. Stir over low
heat until sauce thickens. Add remaining
ingredients. Blend then place in stuffing crust.
Bake at 350 degrees for 25 to 30 minutes.
Serves 6 to 8.

Party Sandwich Loaf

Prepare fillings (below). Trim crusts from 1 loaf unsliced sandwich bread. Cut loaf horizontally into 4 equal slices. Spread one side of 3 slices with softened butter. Place 1 bread slice, buttered side up, on serving plate. Spread evenly with Shrimp Salad Filling. Top with second bread slice and spread evenly with Cheese-Pecan Filling. Top with third slice and spread evenly with Chicken-Bacon Filling. Top with remaining bread slice. Frost top and sides with Cream Cheese Frosting (see recipe). Chill until frosting has set, about 30 minutes. Wrap loaf with a damp cloth and continue to chill 2 1/2 hours or overnight.
Serves 12 to 14.

Shrimp Salad Filling
1 hard-cooked egg, chopped
1 1/3 cups cooked shrimp, finely chopped
1/4 cup celery, finely chopped
2 tbsps lemon juice
1/4 tsp salt
dash of pepper
1/4 cup mayonnaise

Cheese-Pecan Filling
1 pkg (3 oz.) cream cheese, softened
1 cup toasted pecans, finely chopped
1 can (8 3/4 oz.) crushed pineapple, well drained

Chicken-Bacon Filling
8 slices bacon, crisply fried and crumbled
1 cup cooked chicken, finely chopped
1/4 cup mayonnaise
1 tbsp pimiento, finely chopped
1/4 tsp salt
1/8 tsp pepper

Cream Cheese Frosting
2 pkgs (8 oz. each) cream cheese, softened
1/2 cup light cream
green food coloring (2 - 3 drops or enough to tint a delicate green)

Crown Roast of Frankfurters

1 1/2 pounds all-beef frankfurters
1 tsp poppy seeds
2 tbsps cider vinegar
2 cups cabbage, shredded
1/2 cup boiling water
pimiento

Slice frankfurters lengthwise without
separating the halves. Broil (cut sides
up) on rack about 3 inches from
source of heat, about 5 minutes. Add
poppy seeds and vinegar to cabbage;
toss thoroughly. Heap cabbage in a
mound in center of a baking dish. Lean
frankfurters against cabbage to form
a crown. Pin frankfurters together
with toothpicks. Pour water over
cabbage. Bake at 350 degrees for 10
minutes or until cabbage is tender but
still crisp. Garnish with pimiento.
Serves 4.

Gay and delicious enough for a party

– and look how easy!

Fiesta Peach-Spam Loaf

Cut a Spam loaf in two crosswise. Between the layers, spread canned sweet potatoes, mashed and seasoned. Surround with cling peach slices. Top with 2 or 3 peach slices arranged "fan style." Blend a little syrup from peaches with 1/2 teaspoon prepared mustard. Bake in moderately hot oven, 400 degrees, 30 to 35 minutes.

Corned-Beef Mold

1 tbsp (1 envelope) unflavored gelatin
1/4 cup cold water
1 1/2 cups tomato juice
1 tsp lemon juice
1/2 tsp salt
1 12-oz. can corned beef, shredded
3 hard-cooked eggs, chopped
1/2 cup cucumber, chopped
2 cups celery, chopped
1 tbsp onion, chopped
1 cup mayonnaise

Soften gelatin in cold water. Heat tomato juice. Add gelatin and stir until dissolved. Add lemon juice and salt. Chill until partially set. Combine remaining ingredients. Fold into gelatin mixture. Pour into 1 1/2-quart mold. Chill until firm. Serves 6.

Shrimp Ho-Hos

"Ho-Ho" is Chinese for "extra good" – which most aptly describes this Shrimp in Pink Sauce. First clean 2 pounds uncooked shrimp. Pare one medium cucumber. Cut lengthwise into 16 strips (removing seeds) and crosswise into quarters. Drain a 4-oz. can of pimientos and cut into strips. Saute shrimp in 1/4 cup butter in saucepan 3 minutes. Add cucumber, pimiento, 1/4 teaspoon salt. Cook covered for 3 minutes. Stir in 1/4 cup of the world's favorite flavor – ketchup – and 1 cup milk. Stir into the shrimp mixture. Cook, stirring until mixture comes to a boil and thickens slightly. Stir in 2 tablespoons sherry. Serve over hot, cooked rice. Serves 4 to 5.

Just imagine!

Spam Birds

Toothpick thin slices of Spam around your favorite stuffing; brown in hot oven. Serve with garden peas, candied sweets. Spam is pure pork, hence rich in vitamins B1 and B2.

A supper that sings!

SPAM BIRDS

Spam Birds: the supper that sings so you don't have to.

Whirling Frankfurters for those times when you don't have a Frisbee in your pocket.

Whirling Franks

1 pound frankfurters
10 whole sweet or dill pickles
1/2 cup barbecue sauce
2 tbsps prepared mustard
1 tsp horseradish
warm frankfurter buns

Make crosscut in center of each frankfurter and pickle. Alternating frankfurters and pickles, insert spit rod through cuts. Combine remaining ingredients except buns. Arrange hot coals at back of firebox; place foil drip pan under spit area. Cook frankfurters and pickles on rotisserie 20 minutes, brushing frequently with barbecue sauce mixture. Serve in buns. Serves 8 to 10.

Gingersnap Tongue

1 4-pound smoked tongue
3 slices bacon
2 small onions, chopped
1/2 cup gingersnap crumbs (6 gingersnaps)
1/2 cup wine vinegar
1/2 cup brown sugar
2 1/2 cups strained tongue stock
rind of 1/2 lemon
1 bay leaf
1 tbsp Worcestershire sauce
salt
pepper
raisins

Simmer tongue until the little end bones pop out and be sure to save tongue stock. Fry bacon until crisp, drain on paper, and crumble into small pieces. Cook onions in bacon drippings several minutes until straw-colored. Then stir in crumbled gingersnaps, wine vinegar, brown sugar, strained tongue stock, lemon rind, bay leaf, and Worcestershire sauce. Season with salt and pepper to taste and bring to a boil. Boil briskly for 10 to 12 minutes, stirring frequently until sauce is transparent. Take off range, add bacon crumbs and a big handful of raisins. Reheat sliced tongue in this gingery sauce and you'll have 2 days' good eating for 4.

Forget washing out a potty mouth with soap. Just serve 'em this!

Hamburger Melba

1 pound ground beef
1/2 cup instant oatmeal, uncooked (optional)
1/4 cup milk
2 tbsps ketchup
1 tsp prepared mustard
1 tsp salt
dash of pepper
1 tsp monosodium glutamate
6 peach halves

Mix well all ingredients except peach halves.
Shape meat mixture into peach halves. Broil
8 to 10 minutes in broiler or until desired
degree of doneness. Serves 4.

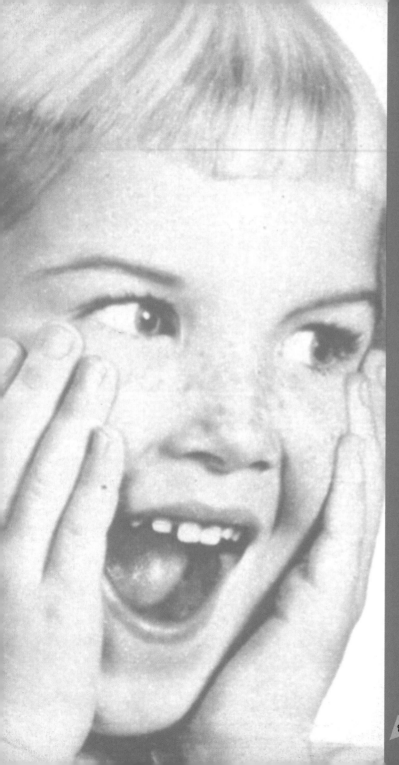

Advertisements during the 1950s:

Ads of this era were filled with messages reinforcing the belief that the way to a man's heart was through his stomach, often depicting the cheerful housewife who had nothing better to do then spend her days and nights in the kitchen cooking up love for her family. The more domesticated she was, the more accomplished she was. It was also during this time that provisions for a more convenient and time-efficient cooking method were introduced. Brands spoke to the suburban housewife with quick and easy meals that saved time but wouldn't take her out of her haven: the kitchen.

82

Kraft Dinner Loaf

Here's a new "quickie" main dish...delicious and satisfying. Use 2 packages of Kraft Dinner. Prepare as directed on the package. (It takes just 7 minutes to cook the special Kraft Dinner macaroni and just a few seconds to sprinkle in fine cheese flavor with the Kraft Grated Cheese!) Pack the hot macaroni and cheese into a well-greased loaf pan. Unmold on a platter, garnish with green pepper rings. Surround with sauce made by heating one can of condensed tomato soup, undiluted. Serves 4 to 6.

Fruit Cocktail-Spam Buffet Party Loaf

1 (15-oz.) can fruit cocktail, drained (reserve syrup)
2 tbsps unflavored gelatin
2 tbsps vinegar
1/2 tsp ground cinnamon
1/8 tsp ground cloves
2 (12-oz.) cans Spam luncheon meat, finely chopped
1/2 cup celery, finely chopped
1/4 cup green olives, finely chopped
1/2 cup Miracle Whip
1 tsp prepared mustard
1/2 tsp salt
5 lemons
Paprika
additional Miracle Whip

Arrange drained fruit cocktail in 9 x 5 x 3-inch loaf pan. In top of double boiler, mix reserved syrup with gelatin, vinegar, cinnamon, and cloves. Place over hot water and stir until gelatin dissolves. Carefully pour 1/2 cup of gelatin mixture over fruit cocktail. Place in pan in refrigerator and chill until gelatin has thickened but is not set. Mix Spam with celery and olives. Mix Miracle Whip with mustard, salt, and remaining gelatin mixture. Add Spam mixture to Miracle Whip mixture and blend well. Spread over fruit cocktail. Chill until firm, at least 4 hours. For garnish, make lemon cups by halving lemons, slicing off ends (so lemons will stand up), and scooping out pulp. Dip cut edges of lemons in paprika. Fill cups with Miracle Whip and sprinkle lightly with additional paprika. To serve, unmold loaf onto large platter and surround with lemon cups. Serves 8 to 10.

SPAM:

In 1959 the one-billionth can of SPAM® was produced. That's enough cans of SPAM® to travel around the world two and a half times! Holy SPAM®! In 2002 the six-billionth can of SPAM® was made. Since 1937, Americans have been hog wild over canned SPAM®, and this 'tasty' processed meat has even been credited by Nikita Khrushchev for saving his Soviet army during WWII. Who knew that Spammy the Pig had so much to give!

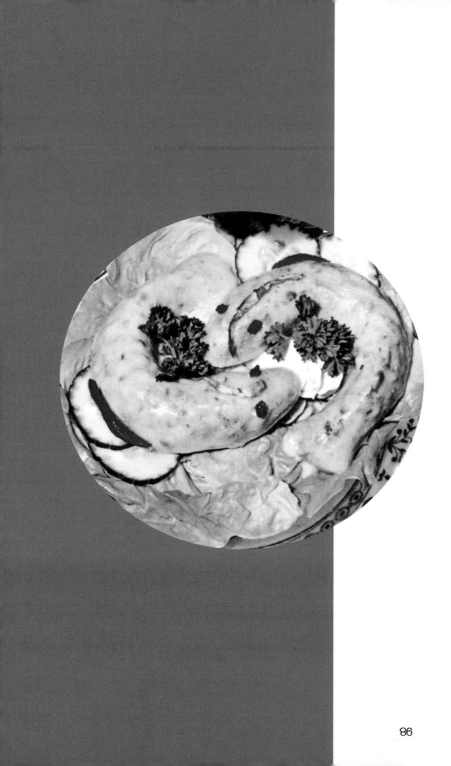

Shrimp-Salmon Mold

1 envelope unflavored gelatin
1/4 cup cold water
3 tbsps lemon juice
1/4 tsp grated lemon rind
1/2 tsp vanilla extract
1 tsp imitation butter flavoring
3 drops yellow food coloring
1 cup buttermilk
3/4 cup crushed ice
6 oz. cooked shrimp
6 oz. canned salmon, drained
salad greens

Sprinkle gelatin over cold water to soften. Stir over low heat until gelatin dissolves. Combine dissolved gelatin, lemon juice, lemon rind, vanilla extract, butter flavoring, food coloring, and buttermilk in blender. Run at high speed until blended. Add crushed ice and run at high speed for 30 seconds. Refrigerate 5 minutes. Combine with shrimp and salmon. Serve as is or allow to chill in two separate molds until firmly set. Unmold on a bed of salad greens. Serves 2.

Soup Cakes! Lunch in 10 Shakes

1/2 can (5 1/2 oz.) condensed cream
  of chicken soup
3/4 cup milk
1 recipe Aunt Jemima's pancake mix
cranberry-orange relish

Place all ingredients in shaker or large
bowl; shake or mix until well blended. Pour
out on griddle; bake these hearty soup
cakes golden brown. For sauce, dilute
remaining soup and heat. Garnish with
cranberry-orange relish and serve.
Serves 4 to 6.

Make this enticing heart recipe with your sweetheart. The perfect couple's romantic recipe: while he cuts the arteries and hard parts out, **you can be preparing the lovely brown sugar raisin stuffing.** After all, the way to a man's stomach is through...a heart?

Set out a 2-quart top-of-range casserole having a tight-fitting cover. Cut arteries, veins, and any hard parts from heart and wash in warm water. Drain on absorbent paper and cut into 1-inch cubes. In a plastic or paper bag, put in flour, salt, monosodium glutamate, and pepper. Place heart cubes in bag and shake to coat evenly. Melt 3 tablespoons of fat in casserole; add meat and brown on all sides over medium heat, stirring occasionally. Add gradually the water, lemon, cloves, and bayleaf. Cover casserole tightly. Simmer 1 1/2 to 2 1/2 hours or until meat is tender. If necessary, add additional hot water during cooking period. Meanwhile, wash, quarter, core, pare, and dice the apples. In a large skillet, melt 1/4 cup fat and add apples, onion, brown sugar, raisins, and water. Cover and simmer 5 minutes, stirring occasionally. Drain meat; remove lemon, cloves, and bay leaf. Lightly mix apple mixture, meat, bread cubes, milk, butter, and salt. Spoon mixture into casserole and bake at 350 degrees for 15 to 20 minutes or until browned. Serves 6 to 7.

Heart With Apple-Raisin Stuffing

2 pounds heart (beef, lamb, veal, or pork)
1/2 cup flour
2 tsps salt
1 tsp monosodium glutamate
1/2 tsp pepper
1/4 cup plus 3 tbsps fat or drippings, divided
1 cup hot water
1 lemon, sliced
8 whole cloves
1 bay leaf
3 medium-size (1 pound) tart apples
1/2 cup (about 1 medium-size) onion, chopped
1/2 cup brown sugar, firmly packed
1/2 cup raisins
2 tbsps water
1 quart (4 to 6 slices) bread cubes
1/2 cup milk
2 tbsps butter or margarine, melted
1/2 tsp salt

When you have too many rotten bananas in your kitchen, don't just make boring old banana bread! Give your kids a real treat with extra-moist banana meat loaf.

Banana Treets

2 cups flour
1 1/2 tbsps baking powder
1 1/2 tsps sugar
3/4 tsp salt
2 eggs
2 cups milk
3 tbsps vegetable oil
1 can Treet or Premium Pork, finely chopped
1 cup bananas, mashed
1/2 cup pecans, chopped

Combine flour, baking powder, sugar, and salt. Combine eggs, milk, and oil; mix well. Add liquid mixture all at once to dry mixture; mix only until moistened. Stir in Treet or Premium Pork, bananas, and nuts. Bake on hot, lightly greased griddle, using 1/2 cup batter for each. Turn when top is slightly bubbly and edges slightly dry. Serves 4 to 6.

Banana Meat Loaf

Bananas assure a moist, savory goodness in this thrifty meat loaf recipe.

1 pound ground beef
1 tbsp onion, chopped
1 tsp salt
1/4 tsp pepper
1 cup soft bread crumbs
3/4 cup (about 2) bananas, mashed
2 tsps prepared mustard

Preheat oven to 350 degrees. Mix meat, onion, salt, pepper, and crumbs. Combine bananas and mustard; add to meat mixture and mix well. Form into a loaf and place in baking dish or fill small loaf pan. Bake about 1 hour or until meat is thoroughly cooked. Serves 4 to 6.

Vegetables & Sides

5

Spinach Timbales

Chop fine 3 cups of thoroughly drained, cooked spinach. Season with salt and pepper and pack into 6 greased custard cups. For the rich cheese sauce, melt 1/2 pound of Velveeta in the top of a double boiler. Gradually add 1/4 cup of milk, stirring constantly until sauce is smooth. Unmold timbales on a round chop plate, pour a generous amount of Velveeta sauce over each, and garnish with pimiento rounds. Here's just one of many main dish tricks with Velveeta!

it's spinach gone boob-alicious and Velveeta makes it neat-a!

Everything tastes better with "cheese" on top.

Cottage Cheese Vegetable Ring

1 cup (8 oz.) cottage cheese
1 tsp salt
1 tsp Worcestershire sauce
2 tbsps onion, minced
3 eggs
1 cup milk
1 cup mixed vegetables, cooked

Blend cottage cheese with salt, Worcestershire sauce, and onion. Beat eggs slightly. Add milk and combine with cottage cheese mixture then fold in vegetables. Pour into greased and wax-paper-lined 8-inch ring mold. Place in pan of hot water. Bake at 375 degrees for 45 to 50 minutes or until knife inserted in the center comes out clean. Let stand about 5 minutes before removing from ring. Serves 4 to 6.

It's soooo weird you almost gotta try it. And if it doesn't taste good, just stick it on your head for a lovely Easter Sunday hat.

Baked Bananas With Horseradish

Preheat oven to 475 degrees. Pour 3/4 cup orange juice into a medium-size, shallow baking dish. Peel 4 bananas and slice in half lengthwise. Put into orange juice and spread 1/2 teaspoon prepared horseradish over each banana half. Bake 15 minutes and serve hot. Four people will ponder happily over this mysterious but good dish.

"If I eat all my baked horseradish bananas, Mommy promised she'd give me some ice cream."

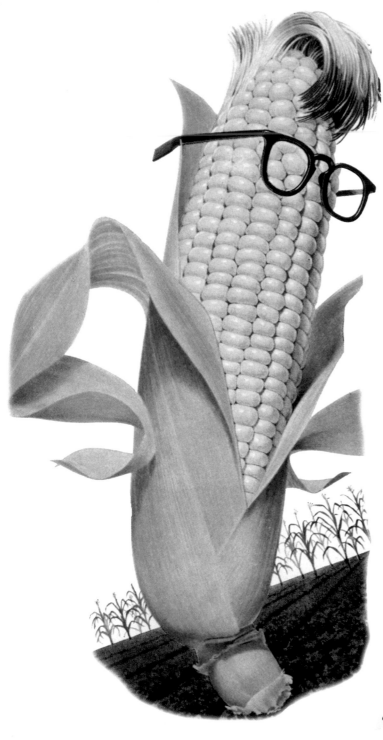

Corn Break-Aways

Bisquick
6 ears corn

Mix 2 1/2 cups biscuit dough according to directions on package. Have dough softer than for rolled biscuits. Pat or roll out to slightly less than 1/4-inch thickness then cut in 2-inch strips. Wrap spirally around 6 ears fresh corn, being certain dough covers ends of corn ears. Preheat broiler and set at 500 degrees. Broil corn for 10 minutes close to heat. Move broiler pan to second rack from source of heat. Reset heat control at 400 degrees and broil 20 minutes or until corn is tender. Remove blanket. Serve with melted butter and salt. Corn Break-Aways have mellow flavor of corn roasted over charcoal.

If you encounter troublesome people when picnicking, Corn Break-Aways also function as defensive weapons.

Baked Corn Chex 'n' Cheese Custard

1/4 cup green pepper, chopped
1/3 cup onion, finely chopped
2 tbsps butter
3 large eggs
2 cups milk
1 tsp salt
1/2 tsp sugar
1/8 tsp pepper
1 cup American cheese, shredded
1 pound canned corn, drained
2 cups Corn Chex, coarsely broken

Preheat oven to 325 degrees. Saute green
pepper and onion in butter until limp. Beat
together eggs, milk, salt, sugar, and pepper.
Stir in cheese, corn, sauteed peppers and
onions, and 1 1/2 cups cereal. Pour into buttered
2-quart casserole and top with remaining
cereal. Bake uncovered for 45 to 50 minutes or
until set. Cool 10 minutes before serving.
Serves 6.

Candied Sweet Potatoes

2 pounds sweet potatoes (4 medium)
1 cup Dr Pepper
3/4 cup sugar
1/4 cup butter
1/2 tsp salt

Parboil potatoes 10 minutes. Place in cold water.
Peel and slice crosswise into casserole. Combine
Dr Pepper, sugar, butter, and salt. Bring to boil
and boil for 10 minutes. Pour over potatoes. Bake
at 375 degrees for 45 minutes. Baste potatoes
several times with syrup as potatoes bake.

Green Bean Supper Platter

1 box frozen green beans, French style
1 tbsp butter or margarine
2 tbsps flour
1/2 tsp dry mustard
1 cup milk
1 bouillon cube
1/2 tsp Worcestershire sauce
1 cup American cheese, grated
4 eggs

Cook green beans per package instructions and drain. To make sauce, melt butter in saucepan; add flour and mustard and blend. Add milk gradually and cook over medium heat until mixture is thickened, stirring constantly. Then add bouillon cube, Worcestershire sauce, and cheese and stir until cheese is melted. Remove from heat. Scramble eggs to creamy consistency and place in center of hot platter. Arrange beans in border around eggs and cover with cheese sauce. Garnish with sliced tomatoes and water cress. Serves 4.

Ketchup, catsup, catchup, what's in a name? Apparently America's favorite condiment! Since the 1800's, ketchup has been gracing the foods of American cuisine. Originally derived from the Chinese word ketsiap, ketchup is now found in 97 percent of U.S. households. According to Heinz, it was a "Blessed relief for Mother and the other women in the household!" (This was the Heinz slogan when it introduced its commercial version of ketchup in 1876.)

Sips & Slurps

Tomato Buttermilk Pickup

2 cups tomato juice, chilled
salt to taste
4 cups cold buttermilk

Combine all ingredients and mix well.
Serves 6 to 8.

This tomato pickup will
have your guests picking
up and heading right out
the door.

Prune Milk Shake

3 cups milk
1 cup vanilla ice cream
1 cup prune juice

Place all ingredients in mixer and
shake vigorously. Serves 6.

if you won't take your Metamucil,
this will get you going straight.

Candy Cane Punch

1/4 cup lemon juice
1 can (6 oz.) frozen orange juice
    concentrate
1/4 cup sugar
1 egg white
6 hard peppermint candies
4 peppermint candy canes
ginger ale

Put all ingredients except candy canes and ginger ale into a blender. Cover and process until candies are dissolved. Divide evenly between four tall glasses, fill with ginger ale. Stir gently to mix. Serve with peppermint candy canes as stirrers. Serves 4.

Add a bottle of vodka to this and create the perfect mock Rumpleminze... it's fizzy, it's fluffy, and oh-so-minty fresh.

Spam Shake

1 can Spam
1 tin anchovies
2 12-oz. cans of beer
4 oz. tomato juice
1 tsp Dijon mustard
1/2 cup parsley, chopped
1/4 cup scallions, chopped
dash of Tabasco
salt (if you'd need it)
pepper to taste

Put all ingredients in a blender and blend until smooth. Serve chilled with celery stick.

The perfect **hangover** remedy: it makes you feel so bad you have to feel better.

Tomato Juice Cocktail

2 cups tomato juice
4 tsps parsley, chopped
4 tsps chives or onion, chopped
1/8 tsp Tabasco sauce
1/8 tsp Worcestershire sauce
1 cup lemon carbonated beverage
4 tbsps evaporated milk, undiluted and
  chilled

Let chives, parsley, and seasonings stand in
the tomato juice in the refrigerator for 3
hours. Strain. Chill thoroughly and add the
lemon carbonated beverage, which has
been previously chilled, and the evaporated
milk. Shake or stir slightly and serve in
glasses surrounded with shaved ice.

Serve with Anchovy Potato Chips. To
prepare, spread anchovy paste on large,
crisp potato chips. Sprinkle very lightly with
paprika.

Pearl Cocktail

2 tbsps pearl tapioca
1 cup grape juice
1/4 cup lemon juice
1 cup ginger ale

Soak tapioca overnight. Cook until
transparent in water in which it was
soaked. Strain. Pour cold water over
tapioca to separate grains. Combine
grape juice, lemon juice, and ginger ale.
Pour into glasses. Add 1 teaspoon
tapioca to each glass. Serves 4.

"Mommy, Mommy!

Can we have Jell-O
every night?"
Sally grew up to be a
6-figure fingernail
model.

Before the
men of UPS,
there was
the local
grocery boy.

Desserts

7

Pop Cakes
Crazy Cakes
Desserts &
Not-So-Sweets

Rosy Chiffon Cake

2 1/4 cups cake flour
1 1/2 cups sugar
3 tsps baking powder
1 tsp salt
1 tsp ground cinnamon
1/2 tsp ground cloves
1/2 tsp ground nutmeg
1 can (10 1/2 oz.) condensed tomato soup
1/2 cup salad oil
5 egg yolks
2 tsps lemon rind, grated
1 cup egg whites (7 to 8)
1/2 tsp cream of tartar

Preheat oven to 325 degrees. Sift together flour, sugar, baking powder, and seasonings in a bowl. Make a well in flour mixture; add soup, oil, egg yolks, and rind; beat until smooth. Beat egg whites and cream of tartar together until they form very stiff peaks. Pour egg yolk mixture gradually over whites, gently folding with rubber spatula until completely blended. Pour into ungreased 10-inch tube pan. Bake for 55 minutes. Increase oven temperature to 350 degrees; bake 10 to 15 minutes longer or until top springs back when lightly touched. Remove from oven and turn pan upside down over neck of funnel; cool. Loosen cake around edges with spatula; remove from pan and frost, if desired.

American Pie: Roll it, pat it, and mark it with an "M". Then put it in the oven for me and my man!

Poke Cake

1 pkg (2-layer size) white cake mix
1 pkg (4-serving size) Jell-O brand vanilla flavor
   instant pudding and pie filling
4 eggs
1 cup water
1/4 cup oil
1 package (3 oz.) Jell-O brand raspberry flavor
   gelatin
1 cup boiling water
1 cup cold water

Combine cake mix, pudding mix, eggs, 1 cup water,
and the oil in a large mixer bowl; blend well. Then
beat at medium speed of electric mixer for 4
minutes. Pour into greased and floured 13 X 9-inch
pan. Bake at 350 degrees for 45 to 50 minutes or
until cake springs back when lightly touched. Cool in
pan about 15 minutes. Meanwhile, dissolve gelatin in
boiling water; add cold water. Poke holes in warm
cake with fork at 1/2-inch intervals. Carefully pour
gelatin over cake. Chill 3 to 4 hours. Cut into
squares and top with prepared whipped topping, if
desired. Serves 12 to 15.

**Kids line up to poke the cake and then
watch Mom drizzle the magic Jell-O fun into
the holes. This makes for a tasty, moist cake
with just the right amount of wiggle.**

Veg-All has been cooking up some fun in the kitchen since 1926. The self-proclaimed "perfect ingredient for any dish" is made up of carrots, potatoes, celery, peas, green beans, corn, and lima beans. While Los Angeles was busy opening its first Disneyland, Veg-All was refining and perfecting its product. Your kids don't need to visit Mickey Mouse. Just whip up a Veg-All cake, and they'll be laughing all the way to the dinner table!

Veg-All Cake

2 cups sugar
4 eggs
1/4 cup vegetable oil
1 tbsp ground cinnamon
1/2 tsp ground ginger
1/4 tsp ground cloves
2 cups all-purpose flour
2 tsps baking soda
2 cans (15 oz. each) Veg-All Mixed Vegetables,
    drained and pureed
1 1/2 cups pecans, chopped

Preheat oven to 350 degrees. In a large mixing bowl, beat together sugar, eggs, oil, cinnamon, ginger, and cloves. Add flour and baking soda, mix well. Stir in Veg All and nuts. Pour into a greased 9 x 13-inch pan and bake for 35 to 40 minutes or until tested done. Cool before frosting.

Cream Cheese Frosting
1/2 cup butter, softened
1 pkg (8 oz.) cream cheese, softened
2 1/2 cups powdered sugar
2 tsps vanilla
milk

In a medium mixing bowl, beat butter and cream cheese until smooth. Add sugar and vanilla and beat well. Add milk by teaspoonfuls until frosting is of good spreading consistency. Serves 14 to 16.

Fresca Cake With Maraschino Frosting

3 cups sugar
1/2 pound butter
1/2 cup vegetable shortening
6 large eggs
3 cups cake flour, sifted
7 oz. Fresca
1 tsp baking powder
1 tsp vanilla extract
1 tbsp lemon rind, grated
1 tbsp lime rind, grated

Preheat oven to 350 degrees. Cream together sugar,
butter, and shortening. Add eggs one at a time, beating
well after each addition. Add flour and Fresca
alternately. Add baking powder and, when mixture is fully
creamed, add vanilla and fruit rinds. Pour into greased
and floured 9 x 13-inch cake pan. Bake 1 hour or until
cake tester comes out clean.

Icing:
2 large egg whites
1 cup sugar
1 tbsp water
2 tbsps maraschino cherry juice
1 tbsp light corn syrup
1/4 tsp cream of tartar
10 maraschino cherries, chopped

Mix all ingredients except cherries and beat constantly
while heating in the top of a double boiler. When
thoroughly mixed – thick and spreadable – frost cake.
Decorate top of cake with chopped maraschino
cherries. Serves 8.

This cake got its citrus zing from grapefruity Fresca. Other pop cake variations include 7-Up, Coca-Cola, Dr Pepper, and Pepsi.

Velveeta Cheese Fudge

1 pound margarine or butter
1 pound Velveeta Cheese
1 cup cocoa
4 pounds powdered sugar
2 cups nuts, chopped
2 tsps vanilla

Melt margarine and cheese together. Mix in remaining ingredients. Spread in greased pan. Cool. Cut in squares. Keep in refrigerator. Makes enough for a big party of six.

Have you always wondered why your sister-in-law's fudge had that extra-special smooth and salty taste?

Apricot Silly Face

1 pkg (3oz.) Jell-O apricot flavor gelatin
1 1/4 cups boiling water
1 cup vanilla ice cream
1 jar (4 3/4 oz.) strained apricots
chocolate chips
chocolate wafers
marshmallows

Dissolve gelatin in boiling water. Add ice cream by spoonfuls, stirring until blended and smooth. Fold in apricots and pour into dessert dishes. Chill until set, about 1 hour. Arrange chocolate chips to resemble faces and use chocolate wafers and marshmallows for hats, if desired. Makes 2 3/4 cups or 5 servings.

Mock Apple Pie

2-crust 9-inch pie
36 RITZ Crackers, coarsely broken (about 1 3/4 cups
    crumbs)
2 cups sugar
1 3/4 cups water
2 tsp cream of tartar
2 tbsps lemon juice
grated lemon peel (1 lemon)
2 tbsps margarine or butter
1/2 tsp ground cinnamon

Roll out half the pastry and line 9-inch pie plate. Place
cracker crumbs in prepared crust; set aside.

Heat, sugar, water and cream of tartar to boil in saucepan
on high heat; simmer 15 minutes. Add lemon juice and peel;
cool. Pour syrup over cracker crumbs. Dot with margarine;
sprinkle with cinnamon. Roll out remaining pastry; place over
pie. Trim, seal and flute edges. Slit top crust to allow steam
to escape.

Bake at 425 degrees for 30 to 35 minutes or until crust is
crisp and golden. Cool completely.

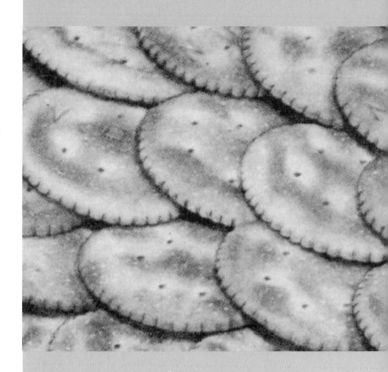

A pie made of crackers –
who would have thought?
But food legend has it that
this recipe will fool almost
anyone into thinking you've
been peeling apples in the
hot kitchen all day!

Often used as a doorstop, disciplinary tool, or holiday joke, Fruitcake gets a bad rap. Having persisted since the times of ancient Romans, Fruitcake is traditionally made up of an assortment of candied fruit and fruit rind, nuts, spices, and usually liquor. And while some Fruitcakes are more edible than others, you'd be nuttier than a Fruitcake to turn one down. It's the gift that keeps on giving!

Chocolate Sauerkraut Cake

Chocolate Sauerkraut Cake

1/2 cup sauerkraut, well drained and finely chopped
2/3 cup shortening
1 1/2 cups sugar
3 eggs
1 tsp vanilla
2 1/4 cups all-purpose flour
1 cup water
1 tsp baking powder
1 tsp baking soda
1/4 tsp salt
1/2 cup cocoa powder
chopped nuts (optional)

Cream together shortening and sugar; beat in eggs one at a time. Add in vanilla and mix thoroughly. Stir dry ingredients together and add to creamed mixture alternately with the water. Begin and end with flour mixture. Stir in sauerkraut and nuts. Bake in a greased 9 x 13-inch pan at 375 degrees for 35 minutes or until a toothpick, inserted in middle, comes out clean. Serves 8 to 10.

This version of sauerkraut cake is prefaced with: "A delicious chocolate cake with an ingredient best kept secret." In retro times, sauerkraut was cheap, plentiful, and made from one's garden. It just goes to prove that if you add enough chocolate and sugar to anything, it will taste good.

Pepsi-Cola Cake With Broiled Peanut Butter Frosting

2 cups unbleached flour
2 cups sugar
1/2 pound butter
2 tbsps unsweetened cocoa
1 cup Pepsi
1/2 cup buttermilk
2 large eggs, beaten
1 tsp baking soda
1 tsp vanilla extract
1 1/2 cups miniature marshmallows

Preheat oven to 350 degrees. Grease and flour 9 x 13 x 2-inch pan. Combine flour and sugar in large bowl. Melt butter, add cocoa and Pepsi. Pour over flour and sugar mixture and stir until well blended. Add buttermilk, beaten eggs, soda, and vanilla. Mix well. Stir in marshmallows. Pour into prepared pan. Bake 40 minutes. Remove cake from oven and frost while still warm.

Frosting:
6 tbsps butter
1 cup dark brown sugar, packed
2/3 cup peanut butter
1/4 cup milk
2/3 cup peanuts, chopped

Cream butter, sugar, and peanut butter. Add milk and nuts; stir well. Spread over warm cake. Place frosted cake under broiler about 4-inches from heat source. Broil just a few seconds or until topping starts to bubble. DO NOT scorch! Let cool at least 30 minutes before serving. Serves 8.

Tomato Soup Cake

2 cups cake flour, sifted or 1 3/4 cups
    all-purpose flour, sifted
1 cup sugar
3 tsps baking powder
1/2 tsp ground cinnamon
1/2 tsp ground cloves
1/2 tsp ground nutmeg
1/2 cup hydrogenated shortening
1 can (10 1/2 oz.) condensed tomato soup
2 eggs

Preheat oven to 350 degrees. Grease and flour two 8-inch round layer pans. Sift dry ingredients together into large bowl. Add shortening and 1/2 can of soup. Beat on medium speed of electric mixer 2 minutes (150 strokes per minute by hand). Add remaining soup and eggs. Beat 2 minutes more, scraping bowl frequently. Pour into pans. Bake 30 to 35 minutes. Let stand in pans 10 minutes; remove and cool on rack. Frost with cream cheese frosting or your favorite frosting.

Wheaties Split

1 banana, split lengthwise
1/2 cup Wheaties cereal
1/2 cup milk
1 scoop ice cream, any flavor
fresh fruit to taste (optional)

Place banana split-side up in
banana-split dish or bowl. Add
Wheaties flakes, milk, and fruit;
top with ice cream. Still your
Breakfast of Champions!

Crunch-ilicious!
"The breakfast of champions."

Another recipe, another adventure... Here's to the next generation!

INDEX